Illustrations by Michael Adams

Nihil Obstat: Right Reverend Archimandrite Francis Vivona, S.T.M., J.C.L.

Imprimatur: Most Reverend Joseph A. Pepe, D.D., J.C.D.

Date: January 18, 2011

Except where noted, Scripture excerpts are taken from the *New American Bible with Revised New Testament and Psalms* Copyright © 1991, 1986, 1970 Confraternity of Christian Doctrine, Inc., Washington, DC. Used with permission. All rights reserved. No part of the New American Bible may be reproduced by any means without permission in writing from the copyright holder.

Library of Congress Control Number: 2011910836
ISBN 1-61796-058-1

Artwork © Michael Adams, Licensee Aquinas Press
Text © 2011, 2012 Aquinas Press, Phoenix, Arizona
First Edition, 2011; Second Edition, 2012

TABLE OF CONTENTS

Introduction..5

God's Dream for Your Family...............................8

What is Prayer?..10

How is *Your* Heart?..12

Hearing God's Voice..14

Spousal Intimacy...16

The Holy Family..18

Family Prayer: Source and Fruit of Family Love.....................20

How to Pray as a Family...22

Praying with Children...24

Praying with Adolescents...26

How to Bless Your Family.......................................28

Creating Memories at Prayer..................................30

Sunday: For God and Family..................................32

Models of Prayer..34

Scriptural Prayer...36

Formal Prayer..38

Spontaneous Prayer 39

Morning Prayer 41

Evening Prayer 45

The Family Rosary 47

Rosary Prayers 50

The Joyful Mysteries 52

The Luminous Mysteries 57

The Sorrowful Mysteries 62

The Glorious Mysteries 67

Blessed to Be a Blessing 72

The Brown Scapular 73

Prayers for Holy Days and Holy Seasons 74

Prayers Old and New 81

Spiritual Warfare 88

The Mass, Our Greatest Prayer 92

HELP! 94

A Final Word 96

INTRODUCTION

"All of us, *gazing with unveiled face* on the glory of the Lord,
are being transformed into the same image from glory to glory,
as from the Lord who is the Spirit."
-2 Corinthians 3:18

One of the earliest pictures my wife took after delivering our first baby was of our newborn son Joshua, staring up into my face. Here we are, this magnificent, pajama-clad baby and his bearded dad, "checking each other out"!

Pope John Paul II teaches us that the essence of prayer is to "gaze into the face of Christ." The first glimpse, then, that we have of God, is the love we receive from the eyes of our mother and father. This gaze ignites within us a delight, a spark, a leap of joy. We are no longer alone. "Another, who is not me, loves me!" And somewhere deep within, our innocent heart responds by looking back, by drinking in the face of this person. This is prayer: Receiving and returning the love of the One who has first loved me.

Our entire salvation is a work begun by God's grace, fostered by His grace, and completed by His grace. What is our part? To cooperate with—His grace! God chose each one of us before the very foundation of the world to be His. Think about that: God wants you to be His, and He wants to be yours. To be fully His, we must be made holy; we need to be transformed. Prayer is the time we spend with God; we cooperate with Him as He makes us new.

Saint John Damascene, in the *Catechism of the Catholic Church*, #2590, states, "Prayer is the raising up of one's mind and heart to God." Prayer is communion with God, who though divine, is still a Person, a Person "crazy in love" with us. But this doesn't happen overnight. Just as we grow, physically, emotionally, and mentally, over time, through a multitude of experiences and relationships, so we grow spiritually. We are transformed "from glory to glory" one step at a time.

In a sense, 'family' and 'prayer' are closely related, because they are both about long-term relationships with those we love. They are about communing together, eating together, walking together, and growing together, with those we love.

As part of our life in Him, Jesus has in mind for each of us a "definite service" which only we can fulfill. Blessed John Henry Newman taught that the believer is taken by prayer into the service of His Master, who alone is worthy of our devotion.

Thus family prayer is more than praying together; it is *living* together in the Holy Spirit. It is Jesus *in* me who is patient when my daughter asks for my attention, when my son needs my help, when my wife could use a break. It is Jesus *in* me—as a father and spiritual leader of our home— who calls my family together for prayer. It is Jesus *in* me who offers to drive my daughter to her swim meet, or who has the unselfishness to save the last piece of dessert for Josh, now a young adult (they can sure eat a lot, can't they?) ☺

This book is written for all readers; however, if you are a parent, as I am, it's especially for you. An awesome responsibility accompanies the gift of our children, and we need help! In this quest, I am indebted to the many authors I researched to compose this text.

In *Family Prayer Book* we will explore together God's dream for you and your family, and how to help you respond in prayer—personally, with your spouse, and as a family. We'll share concrete steps to help you begin or continue praying as a family, as well as suggestions of how you can bless your family. We'll look at the gift of the Sabbath—Sunday—and review models of prayer you might want to explore. This book offers a section on Morning and Evening Prayers as well as a full treatment of the Family Rosary, complete with images, meditations, and prayers for all 20 mysteries of the Rosary!

We offer a section on the Mass, our greatest prayer, and a four-page spread on spiritual warfare, which we hope you will find especially helpful as you seek to protect your family from the powers of darkness. Finally, we offer suggestions on how to maintain or regain family prayer through the trials and challenges that inevitably beset every family.

Most of all, we hope to encourage you to keep reaching for the goal of living happily as a family on earth and living eternally together in heaven. May God, who has begun this good work in you, "continue to complete it until the day of Christ Jesus" (Philippians 1:6). Amen!

GOD'S DREAM FOR YOU AND YOUR FAMILY

Why did God create *you?* Essentially, God wanted you to *be*—and to be His. Saint Paul reveals, "He chose us in him, before the foundation of the world, to be holy and without blemish before him" (Ephesians 1:4).

Just stop and think about this for a moment: Out of billions of possibilities, God chose *you* to be created and He loved *you* from before the foundation of the world! King David tells it this way:

> *You formed my inmost being;*
> *you knit me in my mother's womb.*
> *I praise you, so wonderfully you made me;*
> *wonderful are your works!*
> *My very self you knew;*
> *my bones were not hidden from you,*
> *When I was being made in secret,*
> *fashioned as in the depths of the earth.*
> *Your eyes foresaw my actions;*
> *in your book all are written down;*
> *my days were shaped, before one came to be.*
> Psalm 139:13-16

You are not here by accident, or by chance. You are here by choice—God's choice. He has a plan for you, a dream for your life, if you choose to receive it.

God also has a dream for each member of your family. From His perspective, each of us is unrepeatable. We each have a unique destiny that only we can fulfill, regardless of how the world sees or considers us. Pope Benedict XVI writes, "The most authentic and profound vocation of the family is that of accompanying all its members on the journey to the discovery of God and of the design He has laid down for them." Your family mission is to help each other discover God and His dream for you! Wow!

As parents, we are the leaders of our home. We actually have a decade or so to teach each of our children, followed by a few years to see the results of our work before they turn 18 and begin to move out on their own. Our job is to train up our children to become holy, happy, and healthy adults.

We need to instill true character in each of our children, that they might become men and women of virtue. We need to help them understand that they are spirit, soul, and body—spiritual beings endowed with a marvelous soul and body. We need to help them know *who* they are, and to accept themselves *as* they are—no small feat, for child or adult! We need to help our children set goals and purposes for their lives, and finally, we need to help them develop good relationships—to love others as they love themselves.

Parenting is a tall order—it always has been. But it's also a daily opportunity to start over again! As we raise our children, we can begin, perhaps, to realize that God is also raising *us*.

WHAT IS PRAYER?

"God thirsts that we may thirst for Him."
-Saint Augustine

Prayer is communion with God. God is a Person—a Divine Person, it is true, but a person nonetheless. He wants to communicate with **you**! Jesus revealed to us that God is our Father—Abba, Daddy—who really and truly loves us and who is actively and even passionately searching us out!

Please do not just glide over these next words. Let them sink into your heart: **You matter to God**! Not just in eternity, some day after this life is over, but **right now**—as you are reading this book! God longs to talk to you! God longs to love you. Are you listening? Are you enjoying His love?

Saint Teresa of Avila said, "Prayer is an intimate friendship, a frequent heart-to-heart conversation with Him by whom we know ourselves to be most loved." Like all friendships, prayer takes time. So don't be discouraged if you feel far from the Lord or that He is disappointed with you. The truth is, He desires you and longs to connect to you. Prayer is the daily journey of returning home to our Father, and we need His help!

God created us as an integrated trinity of spirit, soul, and body. After our spirit, the next most important part of us is our soul: our mind, will, and emotions. Jesus is Lord over our conscious and our unconscious as well. He wants to heal every area of our lives, especially our hearts.

Because we need grace and healing in the different areas of our selves—spiritual, mental, physical, and social—we need to pray in different ways. Indeed, there are many different types of prayer: liturgical prayer, traditional prayer, formal and informal prayer, Scriptural prayer, healing prayer, forgiveness prayer, group prayer, contemplative prayer and more.

In addition, there are the many prayers asking the intercession of Mary and the saints. We can pray in a variety of ways, and we can use all our faculties in prayer. For example, there is great healing power in touch, and in the laying on of hands. There is also healing power in singing, in the chants of the Church, and even in laughter. An acronym that may help you remember the types of prayer is **ACTS:**

Adoration
Contrition
Thanksgiving
Supplication.

Truly, only God's Spirit can teach us to pray. He prays in us, as Saint Paul teaches. However, we need words to get us going, especially in families, where we teach our children how to pray. So let us trust in God, our Father, whose power is always available and from whom all good things come. Let us together ask Jesus once again, as His disciples did so long ago, "Lord, teach us to pray" (Luke 11:1).

HOW IS *YOUR* HEART?

"Just because I'm presumin' that I could be kind-a-human,
If I only had a heart."
-The Tin Man, in <u>The Wizard of Oz</u>

Prayer is essentially a *relationship* between God and us. All relationships originate and have their deepest communion in the heart. So, how is your heart?

If your heart is anything like mine, you might have a mixed reaction to that question. Like most Catholic Baby-Boomers, I was baptized a few weeks after my birth. I was raised in a fairly religious family and attended Catholic school through the 12th grade. I was an altar boy, received all my sacraments, etc.

Even so, all my life I've struggled to believe in God's unconditional love for me, since I am a flawed, imperfect person. Sound familiar? I could be holier, more loving, less angry…the list goes on and on. I tend to think that God sees me as I see myself—barely lovable at times and definitely unworthy! How about you? The good news is, God **really does** love us! He sees His Son in us.

> *God does not always rebuke,*
> *nurses no lasting anger,*
> *Has not dealt with us as our sins merit,*
> *nor requited us as our deeds deserve.*
> *As the heavens tower over the earth,*
> *so God's love towers over the faithful.*
> –Psalm 103: 9-13

Think about it: God has loved you from before the foundation of the world!

> *"I have loved you with an everlasting love;*
> *I have drawn you with loving-kindness."*
> –Jeremiah 31:3

When I slow down and just rest in the company of our Lord after Holy Communion or in a quiet place at home or outdoors, His presence begins to find a deeper root in my soul. I experience more truly this reality: *I belong to God.*

> *Do you not know that your body is a temple of the holy Spirit within you, whom you have from God, and that* **you are not your own?**
> *For you have been purchased at a price.*
> *Therefore, glorify God in your body.*
> –1 Corinthians 6:19-20

This means I can let go and let God. I am not in charge; I do not have to run the universe or even control my family—as if I could! God calls me to let *Him* love me, to surrender myself to Him, to TRUST! God calls me to listen, and obey. He calls me to care for my heart, to watch over it, to guard the good He has put in me: "Keep your heart with all vigilance; for from it flow the springs of life" (Proverbs 4:23, RSVCE *Revised Standard Version, Catholic Edition*). Your heart matters to God. God gave each of us our heart, and like a lover He longs for us to return it to Him. How is *your* heart?

HEARING THE VOICE OF GOD

Prayer, like all communication, is a two-way street. We need to listen as well as speak. But how does one listen to God? How does He speak to us? How do we know it's God and not someone else? Here are some principles to follow:

1. God is my Father.
2. My Father has a plan for my life.
> *For I know well the plans I have in mind for you,*
> *says the LORD, plans for your welfare, not for woe!*
> *plans to give you a future full of hope.*
> –Jeremiah 29:11

3. God my Father wants to reveal His plan for my life.
> *A voice shall sound in your ears:*
> *"This is the way; walk in it,"*
> *when you would turn to the right or to the left.*
> –Isaiah 30:21

Our Blessed Mother Mary herself instructed the servants at Cana, and us as well, "Do whatever he tells you" (John 2:5). In the sacrament of Confirmation, we receive the gifts of the Holy Spirit, including the gift of Counsel, which is the ability to know God's Will. A traditional and time-honored way of learning to better hear the Lord is the practice of *Lectio Divina*, hailed by Pope Benedict as a "tool of the New Evangelization." The components of *Lectio Divina* are to read a Scriptural passage, to meditate on it, to speak to God about what He's saying to you in it, and to contemplate the Word–to let it sink deep into your heart.

God speaks to us to encourage us, to build us up, to guide us, and to exhort us. He speaks to us in the sound of a gentle whisper (1 Kings 19:12). He can also speak to us in the nudges and hunches of our hearts, as well as through our spouses and those in authority in our lives. God speaks to us through the events of our world, the signs of the times. Of course He speaks to us in Divine Revelation, which is Holy Scripture, Tradition, and the Magisterium of the Church.

> *"Whom will he teach knowledge, and to whom*
> *Will he explain the message?*
> *For it is precept upon precept, precept upon precept,*
> *line upon line, line upon line,*
> *here a little, there a little."*
> –Isaiah 28:9-10 (RSVCE)

We recommend that you purchase a special journal. Leave the first 10 pages blank as an index. Then number the rest. Choose a special place and time where you will be uninterrupted. Consecrate this special time to God—perhaps after receiving Holy Communion or in Adoration.

Pray to the Holy Spirit. Ask God to speak, and then write down what comes to you. Let your thoughts flow, even in phrases. Don't judge them at this point; just write them down. When you are finished, ask the Holy Spirit to help you summarize in a few words what is being conveyed to you. Go back to your index and record this short phrase. Review your journal daily and your index weekly. Look for any common threads of what God might be saying to you. Pray and obey!

SPOUSAL INTIMACY

Likewise, you husbands should live with your wives in understanding, showing honor to the weaker female sex, since we are joint heirs of the gift of life, so that your prayers may not be hindered.
1 Peter 3:7

Every sacrament has a specific physical sign that reveals and somehow confers the grace it signifies. For example, water reveals the cleansing love of God and actually confers that grace in the sacrament of Baptism. In the sacrament of Matrimony, Pope John Paul II teaches us that there are two physical signs that confer grace: the verbal consent of the man and wife to wed one another **and** their physical consent expressed in the marital embrace of sexual intercourse. Thus in marriage the husband and wife mirror the intense love and desire for union that God has for each of us.

The *Catechism of the Catholic Church* teaches that prayer is the place where "we 'gather up' the heart, recollect our whole being under the prompting of the Holy Spirit, abide in the dwelling place of the Lord which we are, (and) awaken our faith in order to enter into the presence of him who awaits us. We let our masks fall and turn our hearts back to the Lord who loves us, so as to hand ourselves over to him as an offering to be purified and transformed" (CCC, #2711).

It's interesting that the Catechism should speak of letting our masks fall. This is the step which opens us up to intimacy with one another. To drop our masks means to take a risk, which is not easy, especially if we've been hurt, embarrassed, or wounded by someone in the past. If you're in that category, spend some time with Jesus in prayer. Ask Him to heal you and to restore His peace in your heart. Ask Him to heal your relationship with your spouse. Seek to discern the guidance of the Holy Spirit, who speaks to us in our hearts as well as through the Church and others.

Your vocation to marriage is your primary calling from God. It is therefore the place where He *most* wants to give you grace to carry out His Will and fulfill His dream for you. Quite frankly it also the place where the enemy of our souls will aim his most intense arrows in order to keep you and your wife or husband from glorifying God. It is not easy to consistently give of ourselves to our spouses and families. However, it is our road into the kingdom of heaven. Moreover, we are not alone, for Jesus said, "take courage, I have conquered the world" (John 16:33).

It has been said that the best thing a father can do for his children is to love their mother. When you and your spouse enjoy spousal intimacy, God is pleased, you and your beloved are at peace, and your children sense the good. Finally, your shared prayers carry great weight, and believe me, your children, your extended family, and others are in great need of them!

THE HOLY FAMILY

When it comes to families, most Catholics were raised with a model that far outstripped any of the competition—the Holy Family. If you're anything like me, you've admired the Holy Family from afar, but have long ago given up even the faintest hope of being like them. I mean, who else can boast of having Saint Joseph as their father, the Virgin Mary as their mother and the Son of God as their child? Even so, I have come to realize that the Holy Family *is indeed* our model, and Joseph, Mary, and Jesus are neither unreachable nor untouchable.

God Himself is a Family—a Trinity—of Persons who live in total love with each other, and have done so for all eternity. So it is not unreasonable that our heavenly Father should send His Son to live in a family on earth. We know that Joseph was a regular laborer, a carpenter. We know that Mary, conceived without sin, was still a human mother, who worked very hard caring for her family. And we know that Jesus, though divine, had to grow as a human, for the Scripture states clearly: "The child **grew** and became strong, filled with wisdom; and the favor of God was upon him" (Luke 2:40).

While it is true that we are born "bent" (C.S. Lewis) due to Original Sin, it also true that all children are inherently spiritual and gifted in some way. It is a common temptation for parents to focus more on the gift their child possesses than the gift their child is. Here is where Mary and Joseph can teach us by their example and assist us with their intercession.

Mary knew her son was holy—the Son of God. Yet she didn't try to exalt or draw attention to him before his time. In fact, when 12-year old Jesus stayed behind at the temple for three days, engaged in earnest dialogue with the teachers, Mary questioned, "Son, why have you done this to us?" (Luke 2:48).

Jesus returned home and was subject to His parents, showing us that God treasures our obedience to the lawful authority under which He places us. For her part, Mary "kept all these things in her heart" (Luke 2:51). She listened to God and listened to her heart for the guidance and direction she needed to give her growing son. Thus she and Joseph were able to raise Jesus so that He could grow and develop into a mature person before launching his spiritual ministry.

As parents, our role, like that of Joseph and Mary, is to lovingly guide, teach, and train our children, to help them become fully human and fully holy. We are called, as Pope Benedict said, to walk with them on "the journey to the discovery of God and of the design He has laid down for them." Prayer, whether it be personal, familial, or liturgical, is an integral element of that journey, for it is our daily bread.

FAMILY PRAYER: SOURCE AND FRUIT OF FAMILY LOVE

The family that prays together stays together.
–Father Patrick Peyton, OSC

We are created for love—for union. Sometimes that seems so far from our day-to-day reality of home, work, school, and driving kids all over the place! Shared prayer unites us in heart and spirit with Our Lord and one another. Our hearts are connected with the other members of our family. This connection deepens over time and binds us together at the deepest levels. Even when children grow up and leave home to venture out on their own they remain somehow connected in heart to those who remain behind.

Though we may not always be conscious of this deep-rooted love, it is a source of ongoing life to the family. God's grace often pulls us back, for instance, from giving in to impulses of rage or impatience when we get into conflicts with each other. We have a banner hanging in our dining room with the reminder: "Love is patient, love is kind." This love calls us to remain connected, to care for each other, even when it's hard.

Prayer, then, is a *source* of family love. However, prayer can also be a *fruit* of the family's love. A few years ago, one of our daughters came down with the symptoms of spinal meningitis. My wife took her to the hospital where the doctors arranged a spinal tap to rule out the possibility of bacterial meningitis, which can be fatal.

For some reason, the doctors couldn't pull out the necessary fluid from the spine the first time, nor the second. My wife called me at home and told us they were planning to do this painful procedure a third time. Two of our children and I and immediately knelt down and prayed a decade of the Rosary for my daughter. It turned out the doctors decided against doing the lumbar tap again, and released my daughter, who regained her health in the next few days. My children spontaneously turned to prayer because they loved their sister…and the Lord graciously answered our prayer.

Jesus said, "I am the vine, you are the branches. Whoever remains in me and me in him will bear much fruit, because **without me you can do nothing**" (John 15:5). That includes building and enjoying a happy and holy family. God wants to accompany us parents in the joys and challenges of begetting and raising children for Him. And quite frankly, we need Him, for that is how we were created! Remember Adam in the garden? "The LORD God then took the man and settled him in the garden of Eden, to cultivate and care for it" (Genesis 2:15). We were meant to be a team *with* God, from the beginning!

Prayer, then, is an ongoing and deepening drink at the wells of life and salvation. As such it is our source. However, as we grow in grace, we yearn more and more for intimate communion with our Father, with Jesus, and with the Holy Spirit. Hence prayer is also the fruit of our love, the fruit of God's faithfulness to us and in us all the days of our life.

HOW TO PRAY AS A FAMILY

Once you have confirmed and renewed your own personal relationship with Jesus, and have renewed your love for your spouse (neither of which is ever finalized), you are ready to start praying as a family.

Here are some suggested steps:
- **Set a special time.** Keep in mind that you want to create a **habit** of prayer, so pick a time that works for everyone, as much as possible. Of course, as children grow, this may have to be adjusted. For many families, bedtime seems to be a good time to pray. The day is over, and it is time to wind down before going to sleep.
- **Decide on a "sacred space."** This is very important. Jesus had His special places where He withdrew to pray, and we need them as well. Set aside a small table or alcove at which you can pray as a family.
- **Set up a family altar.** Put up an image of Jesus or Mary, or both! Perhaps you might choose the Divine Mercy image. Select some smaller images or icons to set up on the "altar," as well as a candle and the Bible, and perhaps some rosaries, etc.
- **Talk about prayer with your family.** Share that God is a Person who wants to hear from us and speak to us. He is closer than our very breath.

- **Start simple.** Be patient. For instance, you might begin with a few traditional prayers and build to actually praying a decade or more of the Rosary.
- **Give every person a chance to pray out loud.** God likes to hear from everyone, especially the little ones. However, do not force anyone to pray out loud. If someone prefers to pass, you might ask them if you can pray silently for their intentions.
- **Never use prayer as a time to scold or lecture any family member.** Make sure that every one in the family understands that this will not be allowed. Prayer is a loving and intimate communion with God, not a soapbox. If you need to correct someone, stop the prayer, discipline your child, and return to prayer.
- **Don't give up!** Try to pray every day. However, if you miss a day, just pick it up again the next day. One fall doesn't make a failure!
- **Something is better than nothing.** Even if sometimes the prayer time is shorter or not everyone can make it, just by gathering together you will be gladdening the heart of God and affirming your habit of prayer.
- **Use sacramentals.** Bless each member of the family with holy water and light a blessed candle nightly. Use an Advent wreath. Bring home blessed palms and weave them into crosses during Holy Week. These are only a few of the many sacred objects and actions which the Church provides for us. Sacramentals impart grace according to the prayer of the Church and our own faith, and are a powerful reminder of God's abundant favor.

PRAYING WITH CHILDREN

C. S. Lewis wrote, "Next to the Blessed Sacrament itself, your neighbor is the holiest object presented to your senses." In other words, our spouses and children are living tabernacles, emitting God's presence simply by being who they are—a little hard to see sometimes if you're as nearsighted as I am!

My favorite analogy for a family is the Blessed Trinity. I heard it said that Dad symbolizes God the Father; Mom represents Jesus, our Mediator, and the children represent the Holy Spirit. What I like most about this analogy is that our children, like the Spirit, surprise us and bring fresh life into our families. They are often unpredictable, and sometimes we may find their spontaneity annoying; but if we can see their joy and creativity as precisely the gifts God wants them to bring, perhaps we can more readily appreciate them.

In our homes and families we hopefully come to know that we are loved as we are and for who we are. This acceptance frees us to grow daily more and more into the person God dreams for us to be! Sure we will fail and make mistakes—that's part of being human. But in the home we can practice forgiving and being forgiven, perhaps the sweetest of all human experiences. In the home we can begin again.

When we pray together, we show our children how to open themselves up to God. We help them realize, "Hey, God is right here, just waiting to be invited into our lives!"

And of course, as time goes on, we realize He *was* there all along. That's why being thankful is so right. We thank God that He set all this up for us beforehand, that He is with us now, and He will never leave us. We thank Him for wanting our good more than we do! He is always thinking of us. "Thank You Lord!"

We teach our children to pray both with traditional, formal prayer as well as spontaneous, informal prayer. As Catholics we have a special treasury of prayers reaching back to the Old Testament and continuing up to our present day. We begin with the Sign of the Cross, teaching our children that God loves us from head to toe and side to side! We use traditional prayers to help our children begin praying to Jesus, calling on Mary, Joseph, the angels, and the saints to pray with us and intercede for us. You will find many of these prayers on pages 41-46 of this book.

We also pray informally, as my wife and I did recently when our daughter couldn't sleep due to an onset of hives. God promises in His Word: "When the just cry out, the LORD hears \ and rescues them from all distress" (Psalm 34:18).

It is good to introduce children to Scripture by reading them stories from the Bible or memorizing Psalm verses. Pope John Paul II especially recommended memorizing Scripture and praying it through the day. If you do not already pray as a family, begin today. "Seek the LORD while he may be found / call him while he is near!" (Isaiah 55:6).

PRAYING WITH ADOLESCENTS

Social scientists tell us the two most radical growth and change spurts in a person's life are from ages 0-4 and 13-17. Yet if you're anything like me, I am still unprepared for the metamorphosis each of my children undergoes in adolescence. Everything is affected: their looks, language, dress, manners, attitude, relationships, and, yes, even their faith. As it has been said, "Adolescents are teenagers who want you to treat them like adults when they act like children!" ☺

Adolescents question authority, especially at home! They loosen their emotional ties with their parents while establishing new ones with their peers. Questions like, "Who am I?" and "Who am I going to be?" can lead to some pretty eccentric behavior which can surprise even our teens as they seek their true identity, their deeper self.

While exteriorly our teens manifest their "autonomy," inside they actually need guidance and support. They struggle between their former acceptance of their parents' faith and their own budding relationship (or lack thereof) with God. Though this can be a quite difficult time for the family, it is actually a good. God has no grandchildren; each one of us must ultimately come to know Him ourselves. God created us this way, therefore let us as parents run to Him for counsel and consolation as the journey ensues!

Teens tend to balk at formal prayer, which can seem mechanical and lifeless to them. Oftentimes they are attracted to more casual or personal and informal prayer. Like the rest of us, teens tend to pray more readily when they feel God's presence, and to pray less or even drop off completely when they experience "desolation" or times of aridity in prayer.

In short, adolescence can be a difficult experience for your teen, as developmental changes bring about the inner demise of the world they knew as a child. It feels both scary and exciting to shift into the new, adult world. It is only natural then, that our teens would question the reason for prayer…"Does God really answer prayer…does He exist at all?"

- **With your teenagers, consider praying less formal prayers and more personal, informal prayer.**

- **"Wag more; bark less."** Listen to your teens as they explore who God is—or is not—for them. Remember they are not making ironclad theological statements as much as trying to find out what they believe, and why.

- **Don't stop praying!** Your own heartfelt prayer supports adolescents as they grow, as long as your prayer is sincere and true. Your example speaks, whether they admit it or not.

- **Encourage and foster peer friendships that build faith with your teen, even at the cost of some sacrifice to yourself.**

HOW TO BLESS YOUR FAMILY

God blessed them, saying: "Be fertile and multiply; fill the earth and subdue it. Have dominion over the fish of the sea, the birds of the air, and all the living things that move on the earth."
–Genesis 1:28

God loves to bless us! As His first act after creating us, God blessed us, by imparting to us a portion of His creating power. Scripture teaches us that indeed all good things come to us originally from God, and hence are His blessings.

In the Old Testament, God blesses others directly and indirectly, mediating His blessings through His chosen ones—Abraham, Melchizedec, and the patriarchs and priests of Israel. These priests and fathers of families acted with God's authority as they blessed their sons and the people of Israel.

Elizabeth pronounced a blessing over Mary and her unborn baby to open the New Testament: "Most blessed are you among women, and blessed is the fruit of your womb" (Luke 1:42). Jesus has been blessing us ever since! In the Beatitudes He blessed the poor, those who mourn, those who know they are so needy; He blessed children, the loaves and the fish, and in His final act of absolute love, Jesus blessed the bread and wine which became the Eucharist—His Body and Blood!

Saint Peter exhorts, "Do not return evil for evil, or insult for insult; but, on the contrary, a blessing, because to this you were called, that you might inherit a blessing" (1 Peter 3:9).

A blessing puts us under God's favor, or dedicates someone or something to His service. A blessing cancels out a curse. Liturgically, all ordained ministers—bishops, priests, and deacons—may bless us with the sacramental blessing of the Church.

We strongly encourage you to put up a holy water font in your home and to regularly bless yourselves, your children, and others, with the Sign of the Cross. As parents you have the unique privilege of blessing your children, calling down upon them the favor and protection of God. A great example of this is Saint Thomas More, who was blessed by his parents in his childhood home. He continued the practice with his own family, and even as Lord Chancellor of England, Thomas would kneel in the morning for his father's blessing before going off to his duties.

The traditional way to impart this blessing is to have your child kneel. Lay your hands on your child's head, and then bless your child with the Sign of the Cross on the child's forehead while praying: "May the Almighty God, Father, Son, and Holy Spirit, bless you, my child, for time and eternity, and may this blessing remain forever with you. Amen."

Saint Ambrose wrote of this practice, "You may not be rich; you may be unable to bequeath any great possessions to your children; but one thing you can give them: the heritage of your blessing. And it is better to be blessed than to be rich."

CREATING MEMORIES AT PRAYER

> *"Take care and be earnestly on your guard not to forget the things which your own eyes have seen, nor let them slip from your memory as long as you live, but teach them to your children and to your children's children."*
> –Deuteronomy 4:9

A teacher told me my job as a dad was to "create good memories." I have a long way to go! Even so, family prayer is one of those "moments" that will not only remain in our children's memories but can and will profoundly affect them in their everyday lives.

Here are a few of the many instances in Scripture where God exhorts us to remember what He's telling us—to create good memories:

> *"**Remember** to keep holy the sabbath day."*
> –Exodus 20:8

> *"**Remember** as long as you live the day of your departure from the land of Egypt."*
> –Deuteronomy 16:3

> *"**Remember** the word I spoke to you, 'No slave is greater than his master.'"*
> –John 15:20

For the Jews, to remember something meant to actually re-experience it. Thus, the Lord commanded that the Passover would be a memorial feast for the Hebrew people forever. They must remember and in a sense re-experience the power of their deliverance from bondage in Egypt. At his final Passover on Holy Thursday, Jesus tells his apostles, "Do this in memory of me." (Luke 22:19)—Remember Me! In the Eucharist, Jesus makes present again His sacrificial offering of Himself at Calvary, and His giving of Himself as sacred food so all can commune with Him. This inestimable gift makes present Christ's death and His Resurrection.

Our history as the people of God is replete with this command to remember, to memorialize, and to make memories of our times of communion with God, in order that we and our children might recall and re-experience His saving presence in our own lives today.

Here are some suggestions for making memories at prayer:

- **Pray the *Morning Offering* and *Daily Consecration to Mary* together as a family** (Page 42).
- **Pray the *Angelus* daily** (Page 43).
- **Pray Grace at Meals** (Page 81).
- **Pray the Family Rosary** (Page 47).
- **Attend Mass as a family.**
- **Pray in the car.** We suggest you simply pray one *Hail Mary* followed by, "Our Lady of the Way, pray for us." Of course, if you like, you can add more!

SUNDAY: FOR GOD AND FAMILY

Therefore, you must keep the sabbath as something sacred. ... Six days there are for doing work, but the seventh day is the sabbath of complete rest, sacred to the LORD.
Exodus 31:14-15

In his book, *The Sabbath*, Rabbi Abraham Heschel asserts, "The Sabbath, when understood properly, is a gift of freedom." Jesus teaches us that the Sabbath is made for us, a sacred day on which we are to rest and honor God our Father. Saint Paul proclaims, "a sabbath rest still remains for the people of God. And whoever enters into God's rest, rests from his own works as God did from his" (Hebrews 4:9-10). It's obvious, then, that God is serious about the Sabbath!

We who are redeemed by Jesus celebrate the Sabbath on Sunday, the day He rose triumphantly from the dead. In his Apostolic Letter, *Dies Domini*, Pope John Paul II invites us to see each Sunday as a celebration of Christ's Resurrection, and ourselves as the two disciples at Emmaus, who felt their hearts "burning within them" as they walked and talked with the risen Lord Jesus.

What does this mean for today's Catholic family? God *wants* to give us a gift—the gift of His Sabbath presence. We need to prepare for this gift. We need to better understand this gift. Finally, we need to experience and receive this gift, personally and as a family. Time with Him is our greatest treasure!

God wants us to enjoy even in this world the joy of His presence and the rest from our labors. Hence we need to do our best to finish our home and school work and prepare our home so we can ideally enjoy a special meal Saturday evening and usher in the Lord's Day. As the famed Trappist monk Thomas Merton said, "Food is divine love made edible."

In Jewish homes, the Sabbath is a day to discuss the Torah. Likewise, a great way to prepare for Sunday is to read in advance the Scripture readings proclaimed at Mass and to talk about them as a family.

There is another meaning to Sunday: the idea of surrender. We cannot acquire the peace of God on our own. Our own work does not "earn" us God's presence. Rather, God's peace comes as we admit our "powerlessness" to control our lives. Sunday is a time to come as children to our Father and to receive again His healing, merciful, life-giving, and truly satisfying presence. He is our Divine Bridegroom, and we are called to be His true and loyal spouse, looking only to Him who is the fulfillment of all desire.

Finally, Sunday is meant to be a day for others—to be open for ways to sacrificially give of ourselves to the needy among us. As Blessed Teresa of Calcutta—Mother Teresa—said, "Loneliness and being unwanted is the greatest poverty." Reach out to your extended family or those in need, especially the sick, the elderly, children, and immigrants.

MODELS OF PRAYER

"Lord, teach us to pray."
–Luke 11:1

Prayer—communion with God—is absolutely necessary if we hope to grow closer to God and to abide in Him. But it's difficult to pray always. We need structures to help us. Jesus knew this, and hence He gave us the Lord's Prayer—a model for private and public prayer. As Saint Thomas of Aquinas wrote, "In it we ask, not only for all the things we can rightly desire, but also in the sequence that they should be desired."

We can use the *Our Father* as a model for family prayer. One way is to pray it phrase by phrase and invite family members to both share their thoughts and make the prayer personal.
For instance: **"Our Father, who art in heaven."**
- Whose Father is God?
- Where is heaven?
- Do you think of God as your Father? Why or why not?
- "Dear God, we want to speak to You this evening as a family—all of us together. Please help each of us to know You as our Father. Heal the places in us that might feel uncomfortable calling You 'Father.' Thank You that we can trust You."

Then you take the next phrase: **"Hallowed be Thy Name,"** and continue as above.

Another model for prayer is the Liturgy of the Hours—the Church's official daily prayer—including Psalms, prayers, and readings, arranged in a four-week cycle. The General Instruction of the *Liturgy of the Hours* (sometimes called the *Divine Office*) states, "It is of great advantage for the family ... to celebrate some parts of the Liturgy of the Hours ... to enter more deeply into the life of the Church."

It would probably be best to obtain a book called *Christian Prayer*, which is Morning and Evening Prayer. Dad or Mom can lead the Office, and different family members can read the Psalms and Prayers. This is a great way to introduce your family to the prayer prayed daily throughout the Church.

Saint Ignatius gave us another model, called the *Daily Examen*. At night, before retiring, read as a family these five steps:
- **Be Still:** Ask the Holy Spirit to quiet you down and help you become aware of God present with you now and throughout the past day.
- **Be Grateful:** Look back over your day and thank God for His presence and His amazing gifts; try to just let the day's images come to your mind.
- **Be Aware:** Review your feelings, actions, and motives of the day. When did you follow the Lord? When did you turn away? Why? Thank Him for the times you responded to His grace!
- **Be Sorry:** Ask God to forgive you of any sins or failings.
- **Be Hopeful:** Ask God to help you walk more closely with Him tomorrow. End by praying the *Our Father*.

SCRIPTURAL PRAYER

"You will know the truth, and the truth will set you free."
–John 8:32

God has given us His Word! This is a most wonderful gift. Through Scripture we can gradually become more and more aware of God present everywhere, and especially within our hearts. The Scriptures reveal God as a loving Father who loves each of us with an unconditional, age-old love. In fact, God instructs us regarding the Scriptures: "Teach them to your children, speaking of them at home and abroad, whether you are busy or at rest" (Deuteronomy 11:19).

Saint Ignatius of Loyola teaches us a way to meditate and pray with Scripture.

1. **Read the story or portion of Scripture.**
2. **Try to see yourself as being in the story,** either as one of the characters or as an observer. Smell the smells, see the sights, and observe the actions, especially those of Jesus and the main characters.
3. **What is God saying to you in His Word**? How can you put it into practice?

For this type of prayer you will need to get a good Bible—a version easily understood by all. We encourage you to get a Bible you can write in, highlighting favorite verses and making notes on insights you receive from God's Word.

- **Pick a reading** from next Sunday's Mass, the Mass of the day, or some other appropriate reading. Have the family quiet down.

- **Pray to the Holy Spirit** (page 82).

- **Have someone read the passage out loud.** Invite the family members to use their imagination to experience the scene—the smells, sights, and sounds. You might want to invite them to focus on one person in the scene. Try to feel that person's feelings and think their thoughts. See the writer as speaking to you!

- **Reflect on the words.** Sometimes, as in the Epistles, the Scripture is more of a teaching than a story. "What is God telling me?" "Am I listening to Him?" "What does this particular Scripture say to me at this particular time?" After listening to God in His Word, we need to try to discern any practical steps God is asking of us, any resolutions or direction He is giving us.

- **Resolve to do one thing you sense God leading you to do.** It need not be earth-shattering. Just try to follow the leading of the Holy Spirit.

- **Close by asking Jesus to root His Word deep in your heart.** Ask Him to continue imparting His presence to you and your family through His Word for the rest of the day or evening.

FORMAL PRAYER

The Catholic Church spans back to the Day of Pentecost. Praise God! Because of this, we have a deposit of faith and tradition that is truly abundant and full, offering us tremendous opportunities of grace, wisdom, and faith.

Among these graces are the prayers of our Church, some of which are from the Scripture, like the *Our Father* and parts of the *Hail Mary*, and others which have been handed down to us from the early Church, like the *Apostles' Creed*. These prayers, which were written and imparted from one generation to the next, are known as Formal Prayers. Typically these prayers are simply and easy to memorize. Thus we can pray them by ourselves or with others, without the need of books or other aids.

The *Catechism of the Catholic Church* teaches that vocal prayer is essential to our life as Christians. Jesus prayed out loud in the synagogue and elsewhere. When His disciples asked Him to teach them how to pray, He gave them a vocal prayer—the Our Father. Furthermore, our human nature requires that we involve all our senses in prayer in order to pray with our whole heart. That being said, the constant repetition of formal prayers can easily lead to distraction and a lack of zeal. To combat this, we need to pray *from* our hearts with focus and conviction. As Saint John Chrysostom wrote, "Whether or not our prayer is heard depends not on the number of words, but on the fervor of our souls."

SPONTANEOUS PRAYER

*I will pray with the spirit, but I will also pray with the mind.
I will sing praise with the spirit, but I will also sing praise with the mind.*
-1 Corinthians 14:15

Typically we teach our children formal prayers, which they can memorize and repeat. Often formal prayers make up devotional prayers, such as the Rosary. This is good!

There is also a need for informal prayer, sometimes called spontaneous prayer. An example would be, "Dear God, Joey is feeling sick today. We ask You to please heal him according to your divine Will, and fill him with Your Spirit of peace and grace. Help him to feel better and to feel Your love in his heart. We pray this in Jesus' name. Amen."

It is good to pray both 'formally' and 'informally' in our personal and family prayer times. For families, formal prayers allow us all to pray together and help establish a rhythm of prayer, as in praying the Family Rosary. On the other hand, informal or spontaneous prayers tend to spring more directly from our hearts, and are an honest outpouring of how we are feeling in that particular moment. We need them both, for God is both transcendent in His majesty and immanent in His tender love for each of us. He is worthy of all our praise as He sits high upon His throne of glory, and yet He loves for us to crawl up on His lap and share in His intimate personal love. That's why we call Him Father!

MORNING PRAYER

The Sign of the Cross

In the name of the Father ✛ and of the Son, and of the Holy Spirit. Amen.

The Lord's Prayer

Our Father, Who art in heaven, hallowed be Thy Name. Thy Kingdom come, Thy Will be done on earth as it is in heaven. Give us this day our daily bread; and forgive us our trespasses, as we forgive those who trespass against us; and lead us not into temptation, but deliver us from evil. Amen.

The Hail Mary

Hail Mary, full of grace, the Lord is with thee;
Blessed art thou among women, and blessed is the fruit of thy womb, Jesus.
Holy Mary, Mother of God, pray for us sinners,
now and at the hour of our death. Amen.

Glory Be

Glory be to the Father, and to the Son, and to the Holy Spirit; as it was in the beginning, is now, and ever shall be, world without end. Amen.

Morning Offering to the Sacred Heart

O Jesus, through the Immaculate Heart of Mary, I offer You my prayers, works, joys, and sufferings of this day, for all the intentions of Your Sacred Heart, in union with the Holy Sacrifice of the Mass throughout the world, in reparation for my sins, for the intentions of all our associates, and in particular for the intentions of our Holy Father. Amen.

Daily Consecration to Mary

O Mary, My Queen and my Mother, I give myself entirely to you, and to show my devotion to you I consecrate to you this day my eyes, my ears, my mouth, my heart, my whole body without reserve. Wherefore, good Mother, as I am your own, keep me and guard me as your property and possession. Amen.

Prayer to My Guardian Angel

O Angel of God, my Guardian dear, to whom God's love commits me here, ever this day be at my side, to light and guard, to rule and guide. Amen.

The Angelus

V- The Angel of the Lord declared unto Mary.
R- And she conceived by the Holy Spirit.
(Hail Mary...)

V- Behold the handmaid of the Lord.
R- Be it done unto me according to thy word.
(Hail Mary...)

V- And the Word was made Flesh.
R- And dwelt among us.
(Hail Mary...)

V- Pray for us, O Holy Mother of God.
R- That we may be made worthy of the promises of Christ.

Let us pray: Pour forth, we beseech Thee, O Lord, Thy grace into our hearts; that we to whom the Incarnation of Christ, Thy Son, was made known by the message of an Angel, may by His Passion and Cross, be brought to the glory of His Resurrection. Through the same Christ our Lord. Amen.

EVENING PRAYER

Watch, O Lord, with those who wake, or watch, or weep
tonight, and give Your Angels and Saints charge over those who
sleep. Tend Your sick ones, O Lord Christ.
Rest Your weary ones, Bless Your dying ones;
Soothe Your suffering ones, Pity Your afflicted ones;
Shield Your joyous ones, And all for Your love's sake.
Amen. –*Saint Augustine*

O God, come to my assistance;
O Lord make haste to help me.
Glory be to the Father,
and to the Son,
and the Holy Spirit;
as it was in the beginning,
is now and ever shall be,
world without end. Amen.

*Make a short review of the day, briefly recalling with gratitude the good
things that have happened, and repenting in sincere sorrow for the sins
you have committed.*

O my God, I thank You for having preserved me today
and for having given me so many blessings and graces.
I renew my dedication to You and ask Your pardon for all my
sins. In Jesus' name. Amen.

The Memorare

Remember, O most gracious Virgin Mary, that never was it known, that anyone who fled to thy protection, implored thy help, or sought thy intercession, was left unaided. Inspired by this confidence, I fly unto thee, O Virgin of virgins my Mother. To thee do I come, before thee I stand, sinful and sorrowful. O Mother of the Word Incarnate, despise not my petitions, but in thy mercy hear and answer me. Amen.

Novena Prayer to Saint Joseph

O Saint Joseph whose protection is so great, so strong, so prompt before the Throne of God, I place in you all my interests and desires. O Saint Joseph, please help me by your powerful intercession and obtain for me from your Divine Son all spiritual blessings through Jesus Christ, Our Lord; so that having engaged here below your Heavenly power I may offer my thanksgiving and praise to the most loving of Fathers. O Saint Joseph, I never weary contemplating you and Jesus asleep in your arms. I dare not approach while He reposes near your heart. Press Him in my name and kiss His fine Head for me, and ask Him to return the Kiss when I draw my dying breath. Saint Joseph, Patron of departing souls, pray for us. Amen.

This prayer was found in the year 50 AD. Whoever reads this prayer, hears it or carries it, will never die a sudden death, nor be drowned, nor will poison take effect on them. They will not fall into the hands of the enemy nor be burned in any fire, nor will they be defeated in battle.

THE FAMILY ROSARY

When they entered the city they went to the upper room where they were staying ... . All these devoted themselves with one accord to prayer, together with some women, and Mary the mother of Jesus, and his brothers.
–Acts 1:13-14

The inspiration for this book, on a personal level, came from my memories of our evening Family Rosary growing up. I would like to say these were always prayerful, recollected times of family unity, but alas, such was not always the case! However, it's noteworthy that to this day my siblings and I trace our continued unity and (relative) compatibility to our times of prayer together.

The Rosary is the most popular private devotion and method of meditation in the Catholic Church, joining us to God through Mary, our mother and intercessor. In the Rosary we ask Mary, the Mother of Jesus, to pray for us now, and at the hour of our death.

In a special way, to pray the Family Rosary is to invite Mary into our home, into our family, into the most intimate heart of our family, to be with us. Thus it was that Father Patrick Peyton founded the Family Rosary Crusade in 1942, with the heartfelt cry, **"The Family that prays together stays together!"** Father Peyton believed that world peace flowed from peace in each heart and family—and the key was family prayer, especially the Rosary.

How to Pray the Family Rosary

- Give each member of the family his or her own rosary. If possible, have the rosaries blessed by a priest or deacon.
- Set a regular time—usually in the evening, after dinner, works best for many families.
- Set a regular space, preferably around the family altar, with a lit candle.
- Start by praying one decade each evening, and increase to a whole Rosary over time.
- Involve everyone. Let the children lead the prayers or offer intentions, as they are able.

- Make the *Sign of the Cross* and pray the *Apostles' Creed*, while holding the crucifix.
- Pray one *Our Father* on the first bead, three *Hail Marys* on the next three beads for the virtues of Faith, Hope, and Charity, and finish with a *Glory Be*.
- Announce the first Mystery. Pause for a moment to reflect on it. Then pray an *Our Father* on the large bead, ten *Hail Marys* on the smaller beads, and finish with a *Glory Be*. This is one decade.
- If you wish, you may pray the *Fatima Prayer*, (found on page 50), after the *Glory Be*.
- Continue in this way until all you have prayed all five decades.
- To finish, pray the *Hail Holy Queen* (found on page 51). You may wish to also pray some of the prayers after the Rosary, as found on page 51.

ROSARY PRAYERS

The Apostles' Creed

I believe in God, the Father Almighty,
Creator of heaven and earth;
and in Jesus Christ, His only Son, our Lord,
Who was conceived by the Holy Spirit,
born of the Virgin Mary,
suffered under Pontius Pilate,
was crucified, died, and was buried.

He descended into hell;
the third day He rose from the dead.

He ascended into heaven, and is seated
at the right hand of God, the Father Almighty;
from thence He shall come to judge the living and the dead.

I believe in the Holy Spirit, the Holy Catholic Church,
the communion of saints, the forgiveness of sins,
the resurrection of the body,
and life everlasting. Amen.

The Fatima Prayer

O my Jesus, forgive us our sins; save us from the fires of hell. Lead all souls to Heaven, especially those most in need of Your mercy.

Hail, Holy Queen

Hail, Holy Queen, Mother of Mercy, our life, our sweetness, and our hope! To thee do we cry, poor banished children of Eve; to thee do we send up our sighs, mourning and weeping in this valley of tears. Turn then, most gracious advocate, thine eyes of mercy towards us; and after this our exile, show unto us the blessed fruit of thy womb, Jesus;
O clement, O loving, O sweet Virgin Mary.

V-Pray for us, O holy Mother of God,
R-That we may be made worthy of the promises of Christ.

Prayer After the Rosary

O God, whose only-begotten Son, by His life, death and resurrection, has purchased for us the rewards of eternal life; grant, we beseech Thee, that, meditating upon these mysteries of the Most Holy Rosary of the Blessed Virgin Mary, we may imitate what they contain and obtain what they promise, through the same Christ our Lord. Amen.

Prayer for the Faithful Departed

May the Souls of the faithful departed, through the mercy of God, rest in peace. Amen.

THE JOYFUL MYSTERIES

The Annunciation
Humility

Then the angel said to her, "Do not be afraid, Mary, for you have found favor with God. Behold, you will conceive in your womb and bear a son, and you shall name him Jesus."
–Luke 1:30-31

In this mystery God acts to fulfill His promise made to our first parents after the Fall. We meet Mary in the humble home of Nazareth, as she struggles to take in the angel's astounding message. In Mary's *Let it be*, both her own life and the lives of all humanity are forever changed.

Mary had a vocation, a calling, from God. Similarly, God has given each of us a particular calling that only we can fulfill. Let us thank God for the times we have said 'Yes,' and ask Him for the grace to respond more like Mary today.

Dear Mother Mary, we place in your heart today all those discerning God's Will for their lives. Help also those seeking to live out their vocations as best they can. Lord Jesus, through Mary's intercession, please give us all the grace to live a life pleasing to You. Amen.

The Visitation
Charity

Elizabeth, filled with the holy Spirit, cried out in a loud voice and said,
"Most blessed are you among women,
and blessed is the fruit of your womb."
–Luke 1:41-42

We travel with Mary to visit her beloved Elizabeth. Mary gives Elizabeth joy and assistance in her mission, and Elizabeth confirms and blesses Mary in hers. Jesus shows us that even in Mary's womb He came not to be served, but to serve.

Mary and Elizabeth genuinely cared for one another. Do I put my family and friends in first place? Do I take a sincere interest in them? Mary teaches us to reach out and care for everyone who comes into our lives. She is always close to us.

Dear Mother Mary, we place in your heart today all who are faced with difficulties in their families and relationships, who struggle to know and do God's Will. Lord Jesus, through Mary's intercession, give us the grace of a prudent and truly servant heart. Help us to always reach out with compassion and understanding, and thus bring Your presence to all whom we meet. Amen.

The Nativity
Love of God

While they were there, the time came for her to have her child,
and she gave birth to her firstborn son.
She wrapped him in swaddling clothes and laid him in a manger,
because there was no room for them in the inn.
–Luke 2:6-7

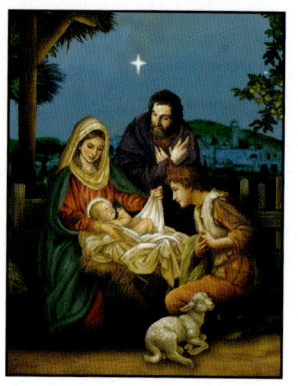

On this holy night the Son of God came quietly into the world to reclaim it for his Father. He came as a child so no one would refuse him. He came in poverty so no one would feel inferior. He came defenseless so no one would feel threatened.

That night in Bethlehem, Mary and Joseph needed help. How do I respond when someone asks me for help? Am I willing to "go the extra mile?" God awaits our 'Yes' to allow Him to come to others. May we share His child-like love, His gracious joy, and His gentle care with all we meet.

O Mary, we place in your heart today all expectant parents,
especially those with difficulties. Lord Jesus, through Mary's
intercession, may we receive Your loving embrace and
share Your love with all who may need us this day. Amen.

The Presentation of Jesus in the Temple
Obedience

When the days were completed for their purification according to the law of Moses, they took him up to Jerusalem to present him to the Lord.
–Luke 2:22

In obedience to the Law of Moses, Mary and Joseph presented Jesus to God in the temple. Israel's long wait for the Messiah was ended. So too was the waiting of old Simeon, who prayed, "Now, Master, you may let your servant go / in peace, according to your word, / for my eyes have seen your salvation" (Luke 2:29-30).

As faithful Jews, Mary and Joseph obeyed the Law of God. Am I willing to obey God, to follow His Commandments in Scripture and in the teaching of the Church, even when it takes great courage?

Dear Mother Mary, we place in your heart today all those in authority as well as those who obey them. We pray that God's dream for each of His children comes true. Dear Lord Jesus, through Mary's help, may we pray in faith, wait in hope, and obey in trust, that You will fulfill all Your promises to us and bring us Your salvation. Amen.

The Finding of Jesus in the Temple
Zeal

After three days they found him in the temple, sitting in the midst of the teachers, listening to them and asking them questions.
—Luke 2:46

On the way home from the Passover in Jerusalem when Jesus was 12, Mary and Joseph discovered that Jesus was missing! Distraught and frightened, they began looking for him everywhere. As the hours turned into days, their anxiety grew. Then, after three days, they found Jesus in the Temple! You can imagine their mixed feelings of relief, joy, and even anger.

We too endure times of suffering when it seems we have lost Jesus. We cry out, "Where are you, Lord?" This mystery teaches us that God is always in control, and that in time, if we keep looking, we will find Jesus. Mary will lead the way.

Dear Mother Mary, we place in your heart today parents who have lost contact with their children physically, emotionally, and spiritually. We pray for parents and children as they struggle through adolescence and young adulthood. Lord Jesus, You who restore all things, please help parents and children to find one another and all of us to find You in the center of our hearts this day. Amen.

THE LUMINOUS MYSTERIES
The Baptism of Jesus
Obedience

Then Jesus came from Galilee to John at the Jordan to be baptized by him.
–Matthew 3:13

John the Baptist looked up to see someone calmly moving down the bank toward him. John exclaimed: "I need to be baptized by you, and yet you are coming to me?" Jesus directed John to allow it, to fulfill God's plan. After Jesus was baptized, the heavens opened and a voice proclaimed, "This is My beloved Son, with whom I am well pleased."

Jesus accepted his mission, and received the power of the Spirit to carry it out. Each of us has a mission as well, that only we can fulfill. Today let us seek God's perfect Will for us, and ask Him for the grace to live it out.

Dear Mother Mary, we place in your heart today our weaknesses, fears, and limitations. Help us to remember that with God all things are possible. Dear Lord Jesus, through Mary's intercession, help us to live out our Father's Will for us, which is our true happiness. Amen.

The Wedding Feast at Cana
Trust in God

When the wine ran short, the mother of Jesus said to him, "They have no wine." Jesus said to her, "Woman, how does your concern affect me? My hour has not yet come." His mother said to the servers, "Do whatever he tells you."
–John 2:3-5

Mary was concerned for the hosts and guests at the Wedding of Cana, and interceded with her Son. In changing the water into enough wine for several weddings, Jesus displayed God's abundant generosity and opened his disciples' hearts to faith.

Whether we are entertaining or just living, we sometimes run out of what we need, and are helpless. It is then that God shows us His unconditional mercy by providing what we need, often just in time. Let us thank God for this gift.

Dear Mother Mary, we place in your heart today all those who suffer from fear and anxiety, who find it difficult to trust in God. Dear Lord Jesus, through Mary's intercession, help us to cast our cares upon You, for You care for us. You will provide all we need, and will open our hearts to greater faith in You and Your undying love. Amen.

The Proclamation of the Kingdom

Conversion

After John had been arrested, Jesus came to Galilee proclaiming the gospel of God: "This is the time of fulfillment. The kingdom of God is at hand. Repent, and believe in the gospel."
–Mark 1:14-15

Jesus preached in the synagogues, streets, and hills of Galilee, offering individuals the fulfillment of all their hopes and dreams. People listened as He told them how to enter this new kingdom: "Repent, turn around, and believe the Good News. God has made a way for you to come back to Him!"

In our search for happiness, we have tried many things—some of which have left us in bondage. Jesus offers us the remedy. But we must repent and believe, that He is the answer, the One who will lead us to true and complete freedom!

Dear Mother Mary, we place in your heart today all those enslaved to addiction and despair, who feel powerless over their lives. Lord Jesus, look with mercy upon all of us in our weakness and speak Your word of truth in our hearts. Help us to repent of our sins and to believe and receive your Good News of true freedom. Amen.

The Transfiguration of Jesus
Spirit of Worship

Jesus took Peter, James, and John and led them up a high mountain apart by themselves. And he was transfigured before them, and his clothes became dazzling white, such as no fuller on earth could bleach them. Then Elijah appeared to them along with Moses, and they were conversing with Jesus.
–Mark 9:2-4

The disciples climbed a high mountain with Jesus. Suddenly, they saw Jesus growing brighter and brighter until he was literally glowing from within! Moses and Elijah appeared out of nowhere, talking with Jesus. The disciples fell down in awe.

How has God revealed Himself to me? How has that moment changed me? Most of our life is ordinary, yet God is transforming us daily from glory to glory, through His Holy Spirit. Am I open to Him working in me?

Dear Mother Mary, we place in your heart today all those who feel abandoned by God, all who struggle to believe in Him. Dear Lord Jesus, grant to each of us a fresh revelation of Your glory, that we may worship You more fervently in spirit and in truth. Amen.

The Institution of the Eucharist
Heart of Thanksgiving

While they were eating, he took bread, said the blessing, broke it, and gave it to them, and said, "Take it; this is my body." Then he took a cup, gave thanks, and gave it to them, and they all drank from it.
–Mark 14:22-23

The apostles had enjoyed the privilege of living day to day for three years with the Son of the living God! Now, at the Passover, Jesus proclaimed that the bread and wine were *His* Body and Blood, given so that He could be with us forever.

Do I ever consider that God knows exactly what I need to live a truly happy and holy life—and that's why He gave us His Son's Body and Blood? Let us thank God again for liberating us from the slavery of sin and death and transforming us through the grace of the Eucharist into the image of his Son.

Dear Mother Mary, we place in your heart today all those who hunger and thirst for God's presence, for His communion, and for His deliverance in their lives. Lord Jesus, through Mary's intercession, help us to often approach Your Eucharistic table with desire, and there commune with You, our dearest and best Friend, the Healer of our hearts and the Savior of our souls. Amen.

THE SORROWFUL MYSTERIES

The Agony in the Garden

Sorrow for Sins

Then they came to a place named Gethsemane, and he said to his disciples, "Sit here while I pray." He took with him Peter, James, and John, and began to be troubled and distressed.
–Mark 14:32-33

Jesus poured out his whole heart, begging for the strength to endure his Passion for us. He placed his full trust and confidence in his Father, as he had his whole life. And in his Father's embrace, Jesus found the power to go on to the end.

Each of us bears affliction at some time in our own life, and we know many who suffer greatly, be it physically, emotionally, or spiritually. In the storms of our lives, when we are betrayed, abandoned, or taken for granted; when we suffer illness, discouragement, or depression, let us turn to Jesus for consolation, strength, and unfailing love.

Dear Mother Mary, we place in your heart today all those faced with trials and difficulties. Lord Jesus, through Your Passion and Mary's intercession may we obtain the grace to carry our cross and to follow You to Your Resurrection. Amen.

The Scourging at the Pillar
Self-Denial

So Pilate, wishing to satisfy the crowd, released Barabbas to them and...had Jesus scourged.
–Mark 15:15

After being betrayed, falsely accused, and imprisoned, Jesus was brought before Pilate for sentencing. His first punishment was a merciless scourging from the Roman soldiers. In his scourging, Jesus was thinking of you and me. He offered all his suffering to his Father to save us from a punishment we could not bear.

Jesus suffered intense, searing pain in his scourging. Do I complain or give in to self-pity at the first sign of difficulty, or do I surrender myself wholeheartedly to Jesus, inviting Him into my distress? Let me give all my sufferings to Jesus, for the sake of His Body, trusting in His unfailing love for me.

Dear Mother Mary, we place in your heart today all those who are persecuted throughout the world for the sake of Christ. We pray for all who suffer from illness, injury, or addiction, including victims of abuse, crime, and war. Dear Lord Jesus, thank You for the suffering You endured for us all, without exception, in Your scourging. Amen.

Jesus is Crowned with Thorns
Moral Courage

*The soldiers ... clothed him in purple and,
weaving a crown of thorns, placed it on him.*
–Mark 15:16-17

The rough Roman soldiers stripped Jesus of his blood soaked clothing, and threw a scarlet military cloak over his bruised shoulders. Then they pressed a crown of spiked thorns down on his head, striking him and saying, "All hail, King of the Jews!" Jesus silently chose to love and forgive his aggressors.

Humiliation is difficult to endure, especially when we are "in the right." Sometimes we need to set our boundaries and stand for what is right; other times we need to "turn the other cheek" and suffer in silence. In all times we need to remember, "Because he himself was tested through what he suffered, he is able to help those who are being tested" (Hebrews 2:18).

Dear Mother Mary, we place in your heart today all those who suffer humiliation and degradation, including victims of persecution and those falsely accused, ridiculed, excluded, or abused in any way. Lord Jesus, through Mary's intercession, grant us the grace of fortitude and protection within Your loving embrace. Amen.

Jesus Carries the Cross

Patience

So they took Jesus, and carrying the cross himself he went out to what is called the Place of the Skull, in Hebrew, Golgotha.
–John 19:16-17

Jesus freely accepted the cross and bore it himself through Jerusalem's narrow and strident streets. Panic attacked him as he struggled to find his footing and fell amidst the shouting and jostling crowd. In their faces He saw hate, rage, and disgust. Saddened but resolute, Jesus kept going toward his final end.

Sometimes our cross seems unbearable, and we panic, thinking we will never be able to complete the course. God will never allow us to be tested beyond our ability to endure. He will always make a way. As Jesus struggled valiantly under the heavy weight of the cross, his Father sent Simon of Cyrene to help him.

Dear Mother Mary, we place in your heart today those who carry crosses of pain, old age, failing in school, loneliness, financial losses, or sickness of loved ones. Lord Jesus, when we feel alone, attacked, or burdened, help us remember You will never leave us nor forsake us. May we always bring Your hope and consolation to others. Amen.

Jesus Dies on the Cross

Final Perseverance

When they came to the place called the Skull, they crucified him and the criminals there, one on his right, the other on his left.
–Luke 23:33

After a brief life, Jesus was betrayed, arrested, tried, convicted, imprisoned, condemned, scourged, crowned with thorns, forced to carry a cross, stripped, nailed, and hung to die. The Good Shepherd went to this extent to rescue his lost sheep, to reopen the gates of heaven and give us all a second chance at Paradise. Jesus thirsts for us to be with Him, reunited with His Father in the Kingdom for all eternity.

Jesus teaches us through his obedience to always please the Father. Prayerful reflection on this fifth Sorrowful mystery can help us prepare for our own passing. We pray that Mary will be with us as she was with Jesus, now and at the hour of our death. Amen.

Dear Mother Mary, we place in your heart today all those who are dying or near death. Lord Jesus, through Mary's intercession, give us the grace to forgive our enemies from our hearts, as You did on the cross, that we may live eternally with You. Amen.

THE GLORIOUS MYSTERIES

The Resurrection of Jesus

Faith

"Do not be amazed! You seek Jesus of Nazareth, the crucified.
He has been raised; he is not here.
Behold the place where they laid him."

–Mark 16:6

Somewhere in the night, Jesus stepped out of the grave with the fire of victory in His heart and an unconquerable joy in His soul. He had triumphed over sin and death. He won!

Although the Scriptures are silent, surely the first person Jesus visited after His Resurrection was His mother, who had been with Him in His life, in His Passion, and in His death. Jesus is also with us, now and at the hour of our death, preparing a place for us, where we hope to go and be with Him forever.

Dear Mother Mary, we place in your heart today all who have died, especially our family members and loved ones. Lord Jesus, through Mary's intercession, have mercy upon our dearly departed, for whom You suffered and died, and bring them with You into the light of Paradise forever, where the sound of celebrating never ceases. Amen.

The Ascension of Jesus
Hope

As he blessed them he parted from them and was taken up to heaven.
–Luke 24:51

After His glorious Resurrection Jesus encouraged His disciples and built up their faith, appearing and speaking to them about the kingdom of God. His final blessing gave His disciples peace, favor, strength, and grace to carry out the mission and vision of the Kingdom. "And if I go and prepare a place for you, I will come back again and take you to myself so that where I am you also may be" (John 14:3).

Jesus has returned to His Father, but is present to us in His Church, in His Word, and in His Sacraments, especially the Eucharist; and in many other ways. Do I seek Jesus' presence as I go about my daily life? Do I live now so as to someday join Him with the Father?

Dear Mother Mary, we place in your heart today all missionaries who preach and minister in foreign lands. Lord Jesus, may those who hear Your Word find the gift of faith and so come to receive the glorious new life You desire for all people. Through Mary's intercession, may we have hope of always being with You, today and forever. Amen.

The Descent of the Holy Spirit
Gifts of the Holy Spirit

And they were all filled with the holy Spirit and began to speak in different tongues, as the Spirit enabled them to proclaim.
–Acts 2:4

After the Ascension, Mary and the disciples were praying together in one place. Early Pentecost morning, a noise like a strong driving wind filled the whole house. Tongues as of fire appeared, parted, and rested on each of them. All were filled with Holy Spirit. Now they could go forth in power!

We too have received the Holy Spirit in our Baptism and Confirmation, yet there is more. We can ask the Spirit to fill us anew, and to release in us all His wonderful gifts. As we live under His anointing, He will produce in us the fruits of love, joy, peace, patience, kindness, generosity, faithfulness, gentleness, and self-control.

Dear Mother Mary, we place in your heart today our Holy Father and all bishops, priests, and deacons. Lord Jesus, please bless all those preparing to receive Your Holy Spirit. Through Mary's intercession, please fill us with the fire of Your Holy Spirit, that He may guide us into all truth, fill our souls with love, and anoint us to bring Your Kingdom to the world. Amen.

The Assumption of Mary

A Happy Death

If we have died with him we shall also live with him;
if we persevere we shall also reign with him.
—2 Timothy 2:11-12

The Church teaches that Mary was taken up body *and* soul into heaven at the end of her life. She is both a sign of what heaven holds for us and a Mother to help us get there. As Saint Paul wrote, "Just as we have borne the image of the earthly one, we shall also bear the image of the heavenly one" (1 Corinthians 15:49).

In the beginning we make our choices; in the end, our choices make us. Mary had a calling, as does each one of us. Am I ready to meet the Lord now? Do I pray for the grace of a happy death? Now is the time to wake from sleep and prepare for the hour of death. Mary will help us experience the truth that "death is swallowed up in victory" (1 Corinthians 15:54).

Dear Mother Mary, you were taken into heaven to live forever, body and soul, with your Son. We place in your heart today the sick and the dying. Lord Jesus, we pray for the grace of a happy death, that we may live in heaven with God our Father and all the blessed forever, where all things are made new. Amen.

The Coronation of Mary

Love of Mary

*A great sign appeared in the sky, a woman clothed with the sun,
with the moon under her feet, and on her head a crown of twelve stars.*
–Revelation 12:1

The Rosary begins with Isaiah's sign: *The virgin shall be with child, and bear a son*, and ends by encouraging us to look to Mary, the *woman clothed with the sun*. Mary is not only Mother, but also Queen of the Universe, reigning now with her Son, rewarded by God for being His most faithful disciple.

Mary's mission endures until the end of time, to mother all of us, her children, through our lives on earth and into our true home in heaven. Let us consecrate ourselves to Mary and ask her help in doing whatever Jesus tells us.

Dear Mother Mary, your "Yes" to the Angel Gabriel set in motion the events of our salvation, leading to our final victory in Christ. We place in your heart today the needs of the Church throughout the world. Lord Jesus, help us to love Mary and stay close to her forever as she faithfully leads us to You. Amen.

...and he will reign forever and ever.
Revelation 11:15

BLESSED TO BE A BLESSING

As shared earlier in this book, my father did his best to lead us in the nightly Family Rosary, with varying success. One night as he was preparing to begin, my next-door-neighbor and best friend, Arnie, knocked on the door. Now, Arnie was a Catholic, as were many of the kids in our 1950's neighborhood. However, my sisters and I were positive that we were the only family on the block that actually knelt down and prayed the Rosary. "Come in, come in!" my dad chimed out heartily. "Go away, go away," I whispered furtively, "or my dad will make you say the Rosary with us!" But it was too late. My dad was already leading Arnie into our front room where the family altar was ready with the candle burning.

Somehow we made it through the Rosary, with much snickering and squirming on our part. I thought I would die of embarrassment. Over the ensuing years, Arnie joined us again, as did other kids in the neighborhood. They told us, years later, how much it meant to them to pray with my Dad.

God blesses us so that we can bless others. Jesus said as much in commanding us to love one another as *He* has loved us. One way is to actually invite others to pray with you. Another way is to pray with family and friends before they leave your home. A good way to do this is to join hands and pray one *Our Father*, *Hail Mary*, and *Glory Be*, and then ask if anyone has any needs. Close with the *Prayer to Saint Michael* (page 91) and the *Guardian Angel Prayer* (page 42). Be a blessing!

THE BROWN SCAPULAR

According to tradition, over 700 years ago Our Blessed Mother appeared to Saint Simon Stock, holding out to him a brown woolen scapular. "Receive, my beloved son, the Scapular of thy Order, as a distinctive sign of my Confraternity. Whoever dies invested with this Scapular shall be preserved from the eternal flames. It is a sign of salvation, a sure safeguard in danger, a pledge of peace and of my special protection until the end of the ages."

The Brown Scapular, then, is a special garment worn as a sign of love and devotion to Mary our Mother and Queen. It consists of two small pieces of cloth, typically wool, connected by two long cords worn over the head and resting on the shoulders. We are called to wear the scapular continuously, to observe chastity according to our state in life, and to pray daily the *Little Office of the Blessed Virgin Mary* or:

- Observe the fasts of the Church.
- Pray five decades of the Holy Rosary.
- Do a good work with the permission of a priest.

Pope John Paul II wrote: "The most genuine form of devotion to the Blessed Virgin, expressed by the humble sign of the Scapular, is consecration to her Immaculate Heart."
To wear the brown scapular is to trust in Our Lady, who has great power of intercession before her Son, and to receive her continuous protection.

PRAYERS FOR HOLY DAYS AND HOLY SEASONS

They devoted themselves to the teaching of the apostles and to the communal life, to the breaking of the bread and to the prayers.
–Acts 2:42

Our worship as Catholic Christians follows an annual cycle of the mysteries in the lives of Jesus and Mary, along with feasts of the angels and the saints, known as the Liturgical Year. It seems that God gives special graces corresponding to these feasts, as He did of old for the feasts of Israel.

We suggest you tie your family prayer to the liturgical seasons, many of which correspond to our cultural holidays. This is a great opportunity to build family traditions that can nourish your children and be handed on to succeeding generations. We encourage you to change the colors of your family altar coverings and add candles or sacramentals of the season.

ADVENT

In **Advent** we remember Jesus' first coming and prepare for His Second Coming. Advent's color is **violet.** Set up an Advent Wreath with four candles representing the four weeks of Advent. Three of the candles are purple, reminding us to pray and offer up little sacrifices to help prepare the way for Jesus. The third candle is rose, reminding us to be joyful since the birth of Jesus is drawing near.

Put up an Advent Calendar—with 24 numbered flaps concealing a bible scene and Scriptural prophecy or verse—on the prayer table or wall. Let each family member take a turn opening a new door and reading the verse as Christmas draws near.

CHRISTMAS

Christmas is the most wonderful time of the year! Replace the Advent candles with white ones and place a Christ Candle in the middle. Light the wreath daily during the Christmas season, which lasts until the Baptism of the Lord. Pray a blessing over your Christmas tree and set up a Nativity scene or crèche underneath it.

Many cultures honor the wonderful feast of **Epiphany** by blessing their homes with blessed chalk, inscribing over their front door the first two numerals of the year followed by ✢ C ✢ M ✢ B ✢ and the last two numerals. The letters CMB stand for the names of the Magi: Caspar, Melchior and Balthasar. They also represents the Latin prayer: ***Christus Mansionem Benedicat***—'May Christ bless this dwelling!'

LENT

Lent, the next major season of the Church year, begins with Ash Wednesday. In this 40-day "retreat," we are called to open our hearts more deeply to God's fervent love through the ancient practices of prayer, fasting and abstinence, and almsgiving. This would be a great time to pray especially with Scripture, as well as to receive the Sacrament of Reconciliation together as a family in preparation for the celebration of Christ's Passion, Death, and Resurrection.

"Blessed are those who consider the poor" (Psalm 41:1). Jesus calls us to care for the poor with material blessings given from our heart. A great family project would be to put money saved by fasting during Lent into a "bank" and then give it to the poor.

Pretzels in the shape of two arms folded in prayer are a traditional Lenten food. Here's a recipe for all to share:
1 cake yeast; 1-1/2 cups warm water; 1 teaspoon salt; 1 tablespoon sugar; cups of flour, (1/2 whole wheat, 1/2 unbleached).

Dissolve the yeast into the warm water, then add the salt and sugar. Blend in the flour mixture. Knead dough until smooth. Cut into small pieces. Roll into ropes, and twist into pretzel shape. Place on lightly greased cookie sheets. Brush pretzel with 1 beaten egg. Sprinkle with coarse salt. Bake immediately at 425° for 12 to 15 minutes. Enjoy!

EASTER!

Easter is the premier feast of our faith. He is risen, as He said! Alleluia! Here are some ways to celebrate the "definitive victory" of Christ Jesus over every difficulty, sin, illness, and challenge we face.

- **Bless your Easter Foods:** (Bring your foods to church or pray over the basket yourself.)

Dear Heavenly Father, we thank and praise You for the joy You have given all people in the glorious Resurrection of Your Son, Jesus. Please bless, O Lord, this Easter food that it may promote the health of our bodies, joy of our souls, and sanctification of our spirits. Please also bless all with whom we share this Easter food, through Christ Jesus our Risen Lord. Amen. Alleluia!

- Light a Christ candle for the Easter season.
- Pray the Regina Coeli instead of the Angelus

Regina Coeli (Queen of Heaven)

V. O Queen of Heaven, rejoice, Alleluia!
R. For He whom you were made worthy to bear, Alleluia!

V. Has risen, as He said, Alleluia!
R. Pray for us to God, Alleluia!

V. Rejoice and be glad, O Virgin Mary, Alleluia!
R. Because the Lord is truly risen, Alleluia!

Let us pray:
O God, who by the Resurrection of Your Son, our Lord Jesus Christ, granted joy to the whole world: grant, we beg You, that through the intercession of the Virgin Mary, His Mother, we may lay hold of the joys of eternal life. Through the same Christ our Lord. Amen.

PENTECOST

Pentecost is the Jewish harvest festival commemorating the giving of the Law on Mount Sinai. On Pentecost, God sent forth His Spirit upon Mary and the apostles, fulfilling the Old Law and giving us a new and living way into His Kingdom. Pentecost ends the Easter season and ushers us into the rest of the year with the dynamite power of the Holy Spirit!

*"If you love me, you will keep my commandments.
And I will ask the Father, and he will give you another Advocate
to be with you always, the Spirit of truth."*
John 14:15-17

Prayer for the Gifts of the Spirit

Lord and Giver of Life, Father of the Poor, You who pour forth Your Sevenfold gifts through the Sacrament of Confirmation, hear us as we pray: Spirit of sonship, grant to us **Fear of the Lord** that we might stand in Your presence with wonder and awe, and **Piety** to draw our hearts to recognize that You are our Father and we are Your children. Keep us in step with You by sending us **Counsel** to know Your Will for our lives, **Wisdom** to apply that Will, and **Fortitude** to do Your Will.

Dear Holy Spirit, beloved of our soul and inner flame that keeps us warm and loving, grant us **Knowledge** to know Your truth in our heart, and **Understanding** to comprehend what You have revealed. Heavenly Father, may these gifts conform us to the image of your Son, Jesus, the firstborn among many. In Jesus' name we pray. Amen.

PRAYERS OLD AND NEW

Family Prayer

God made us a family.
We need one another.
We love one another.
We forgive one another.
We work together.
We play together.
We worship together.
Together we learn God's Word.
Together we grow in Christ.
Together we love all people.
Together we serve our God.
Together we hope for Heaven.
These are our hopes.
Help us obtain them, Father,
through Jesus Your Son,
Our Lord. Amen.

Grace Before Meals

Bless us, O Lord, and these Thy gifts, which we are about to receive from Thy bounty, through Christ our Lord. Amen.

Grace After Meals

We give You thanks, O Lord, for these and all Thy gifts, which we have received from Thy bounty, through Christ our Lord. Amen.

Come Holy Spirit

Come, Holy Spirit, fill the hearts of Your faithful,
and enkindle in us the fire of Your divine Love.
Send forth Your Spirit and we shall be created,
and You shall renew the face of the earth.

Let us pray: O God, who by the light of Your Holy Spirit, has instructed the hearts of Your faithful, grant us in the same Spirit to be truly wise and ever to rejoice in His consolation, through the same Christ our Lord. Amen.

Prayer for Family Healing

Dear God, thank You for the gift of our family. You have called us to love one another, yet we are tempted to fight, bicker, and be selfish. Give us Your presence today and the gift of Your Holy Spirit. Make us instruments of Your peace. Help us to love and serve one another in humility.

Help us to listen to one another, to share, and to confront when necessary. Remind us that growth is a process that takes time and patience. Help us encourage one another to be all You created us to be. We trust in You and surrender ourselves and our family to You, confident that You will work out all things to the good for those who are called according to Your purpose. We ask this in Jesus' name. Amen.

Slow Me Down Lord

Ease the pounding of my heart by the quieting of my mind. Steady my hurried pace. Give me, amidst the day's confusion, the calmness of the everlasting hills.

Break the tensions of my nerves and muscles with the soothing music of singing streams that live in my memory. Help me to know the magical, restoring power of sleep. Teach me the art of taking "minute vacations" ... slowing down to look at a flower, to chat with a friend, to read a few lines from a good book.

Remind me of the fable of the hare and the tortoise; that the race is not always to the swift; that there is more to life than measuring its speed.

Let me look up at the branches of the towering oak and know that it grew slowly and well. Inspire me to send my own roots down deep into the soil of life's endearing values ... that I may grow toward the stars of my greater destiny.

Slow me down, Lord.

—Wilfred Arlan Peterson

The Serenity Prayer

GOD, grant me the Serenity
to accept the things
I cannot change,
Courage to change the
things I can, and the
Wisdom to know the difference.

Living ONE DAY AT A TIME;
Enjoying one moment at a time;
Accepting hardship as the
pathway to peace.
Taking, as He did, this
sinful world as it is,
not as I would have it.
Trusting that He will make
all things right if I
surrender to His Will;

That I may be reasonably happy
in this life, and supremely
happy with Him forever in
the next. Amen.

–Reinhold Neibuhr

Forgiveness Prayer

Be kind to one another, compassionate, forgiving one another
as God has forgiven you in Christ.
—Ephesians 4:32

To forgive others, we must first experience God's forgiveness ourselves. Receive the compassionate, free forgiveness of the Crucified, and thus strengthened, seek to forgive those who have hurt you. Only Jesus can help us to forgive others unconditionally, as He does. We need to let go of our desire for revenge and "paybacks." Often physical healing will accompany our forgiveness, as we release this burden from ourselves unto the Lord.

Dear Jesus, I admit to You that I feel angry and resentful toward (*name*). They hurt me, whether they intended to or not, and I feel defensive. To be honest, I'm not sure I trust this person anymore.

Yet I know You call me to forgive. When I look at Your Cross, I think of how many times You have forgiven me and wiped the slate clean. I think of how often You have given me a new chance, a fresh beginning.

O Jesus, please come into my heart and heal me. For my part, I forgive this person as You have forgiven me. I ask You to bless them and heal them as well. Thank You, Lord, that You alone are the answer to our deepest needs. Amen.

Psalm 23

The Lord is my shepherd; I shall not want.

He makes me lie down in green pastures; He leads me beside the still waters. He restores my soul. He leads me in the paths of righteousness for His name's sake.

Yea, though I walk through the valley of the shadow of death, I will fear no evil: for You are with me; Your rod and Your staff, they comfort me.

You prepare a table before me in the presence of my enemies. You anoint my forehead with oil; my cup overflows.

Surely goodness and mercy shall follow me all the days of my life; and I will dwell in the house of the Lord forever.

Prayer for Healing

O Heavenly Father, God of Love, You gave us Your Son Jesus to be not only Physician of our souls but Healer of our bodies and minds as well. Lord Jesus, I turn to You in this time of illness. Please come to me now, and lay Your healing hands on me. Let the warmth, peace, and healing power of Your Spirit fill me now with Your life and love. I receive You, Lord Jesus! Heal me according to Your Divine Will, Lord Jesus, and enable me to serve You with a healthy body, soul, and spirit. May Your Joy, O Lord, be my strength this day. Amen.

Ancient Prayer to the Virgin Mary

We turn to you for protection, holy Mother of God.
Listen to our prayers, and help us in our needs.
Save us from every danger, O glorious and blessed Virgin.

Healing Prayer for Others
Based on the prayer of a 7th Century Irish Monk

Heavenly Father, Creator of the universe, and Author of its laws, You can bring the dead back to life, and heal those who are sick. We pray for our sick brothers and sisters that they may feel Your hand upon them, renewing their bodies and refreshing their souls. Show to them the affection in which You hold all Your creatures, and grant them an early recovery. In Jesus' name. Amen.

"Pray, Hope, and Don't Worry!"
–Saint Padre Pio of Pietrelcina

SPIRITUAL WARFARE

For our struggle is not with flesh and blood but with the principalities, with the powers, with the world rulers of this present darkness, with the evil spirits in the heavens. Therefore, put on the armor of God, that you may be able to resist on the evil day and, having done everything, to hold your ground.
—Ephesians 6:12-13

Indeed, the Son of God was revealed to destroy the works of the devil.
—1 John 3:8

In the beginning, God created all the angels, including Lucifer, as good. However, through his free choice, Satan turned from God and fell from grace, taking many angels with him. These dark spirits wage war constantly upon us, to try to get us to turn from God and His friendship.

God created every person in our family to grow spiritually, mentally, physically, and socially. The enemy wants us to wither and die. Jesus came to destroy the devil's works, and to give us life—true and eternal life.

The devil bends his attacks especially on families, because we are the domestic church, the cells which make up the larger Body of Christ. He aims at the heart of the family, which is the marriage bond of the husband and wife. He also tries to divide children from their parents and from one another. There are no options in this war. We either fight or die, as Father John Corapi, a popular speaker, has noted. He claims that spiritual warfare is "one of the most consistent and important themes of the Church's preaching and teaching."

When we pray as a family, we are helping to bring forth the Kingdom of God and defeat the enemy of our souls. God wants us to be spiritually protected from Satan. Saint Paul therefore urges us in his letter to the Ephesians to put on the whole armor of salvation. We need to regularly pray protection over ourselves, our loved ones, and our possessions. Moreover, we go on the offensive by praying as a family, and by living a life pleasing to God. This combination will help bring others to Christ.

You may be suprised to learn that we are actually engaging in spiritual warfare when we worship at Mass. As Scott Hahn notes in his book, *The Lamb's Supper*, here again we have a choice: Fight or Flight. He asserts that many people today escape reality through various means because of "the enormity of evil" present in so many places. Yet Jesus faced this very evil for us definitively in His Passion, Death, and Resurrection, and He gives us the power to overcome it. In fact, Jesus calls us to not only overcome evil but to help others also experience His victory.

How do we do this? Here are some classic tools:

- **Humility.** We cannot win this battle in our own strength. In his book, *The Fulfillment of All Desire,* Ralph Martin asserts, "All the saints have come to know this profound and fundamental truth: that the purpose of our life is the glory of heaven, and **the only way to reach the goal is by absolute confidence in God.**"

- **The Rosary and the Scapular:** Our Blessed Mother told Saint Dominic: "One day through the Rosary and the Scapular I will save the world." Mary has repeated her plea at Lourdes, Fatima, and elsewhere, calling us, her beloved children, to pray for the conversion of the world.

- **Prayer and Fasting:** Adding a sacrifice to your prayer is especially helpful in difficult matters. It can be a simple fast of bread and water, or abstaining from coffee, dessert, etc., in order to focus more intently on Jesus.

- **Regular reception of the Sacraments, especially Holy Eucharist and Reconciliation:** Keep up your strength!

- **Reading God's Word daily:** There's a reason why Holy Scripture is called *the Sword of the Spirit*. Use it with confidence. You are His warrior!

The light shines in the darkness,
and the darkness has not overcome it.
John 1:5

The LORD lives! Blessed be my rock!
Exalted be God, my savior!
O God who granted me vindication ...
and preserved me from my enemies,
Truly you have exalted me above my adversaries,
from the violent you have rescued me.
-Psalm 18:47-49

Prayer to Saint Michael the Archangel

Saint Michael, the Archangel, defend us in battle. Be our safeguard against the wickedness and snares of the devil. May God rebuke him, we humbly pray; and do you, O Prince of the heavenly host, by the power of God, cast into hell Satan and all the evil spirits, who wander through the world seeking the ruin of souls. Amen.

Spiritual Armor Prayer
Adapted from Ephesians 6:10-18

Pray this Prayer Daily

Heavenly Father, we ask You today for Your truth as a belt tight around the loins of our mind. We put on the zeal to announce Your good news of peace as shoes for our feet.
We put on Your righteousness, O Christ, as our breastplate, and the hope of salvation as a helmet for our head.

Father, we take up faith as a shield which is able to put out all the fiery darts of the enemy, and the sword of the Spirit, which is Your Word, O Lord. Father, may the love with which You have loved Jesus be in us, and may Jesus be in us. We ask You for the grace of a servant heart. Amen.

THE MASS, OUR GREATEST PRAYER

In this is love: not that we have loved God,
but that he loved us and sent his Son as expiation for our sins.
–1 John 4:10

The Mass is really a love story between a God so in love with His Son that He cannot take His eyes off Him, yet so in love with us that He sends this Son to become one of us and die for us on a cross outside Jerusalem over 2,000 years ago.

In the Mass we return again to Calvary, to the Cross, where our salvation was won in an epic and horrific battle between the Son of God and Satan, as to who would finally have dominion over God's most precious creation on earth: man and woman. Jesus, our divine-human Lover, paid the full price for our salvation; He ended the dominion of sin and re-opened the gates of heaven. God and man could finally be reunited, and the Holy Spirit could be given.

In the Holy Eucharist, Jesus has provided a way for all people, for all time, to come in spirit to the sacrifice of Calvary, to offer that same sacrifice to the Father, and to receive the Body and Blood of Christ for their nourishment, strength, and consolation as they make their return journey to the Father.

That being said, it can be difficult to keep ourselves and our children engaged in worship during Mass. In his book, *The Lamb's Supper*, Scott Hahn offers some insights. We present them here for you:

- **We are actually engaging in spiritual warfare when we worship at Mass.** Hence we shouldn't be too surprised when it seems to be especially difficult on Sundays to get everyone going and to church on time!

- **Recollect at least yourself and if possible your family by arriving before Mass** to spend some quiet time in prayer. Pray for the celebrant; ask the Lord to give him the grace to bring all of us closer to God. Pray for all who serve: the lectors, altar servers, ushers, music ministry, etc.

- **Remember that the angels—millions of them—are present in force at every liturgy,** as are the saints, our heavenly allies. Sing and pray with confidence and enthusiasm!

- **Be aware of the power invested in the sacramentals and rituals of Holy Mass,** such as blessing yourself with holy water.

- **Realize the devil will try to distract you at Mass** through a variety of tactics: boredom, judgmentalism, human respect, pride, and even lust. Resist him, steadfast in the faith.

It can be pretty challenging to keep yourself and every member of your family fully engaged at Sunday Mass. Thankfully, God helps us and He works even in our weaknesses. Just showing up at least ensures that your family is surrounded by grace, and when you worship together, whether you realize or not, your example alone has a tremendous, if not readily apparent, effect on your children. "The family that prays together stays together," and the Mass is our greatest prayer. Rejoice in the Lord and don't give up!

HELP!

A priest once told me, "You will find the cross in the very center of your vocation." When you consider that a father's example is the most telling ingredient in his child's faith life, or that "the future of humanity passes by way of the family," (Pope John Paul II), you should not be dismayed when your attempts at family prayer go awry or even seem to fail. Try not to take it personally when your best efforts seem sometimes only to cause arguments or division in the family. Take heart! Here are some practical solutions:

- **Review your scheduled prayer time.** Maybe it's too late, or too early! As family schedules change, it may be necessary to revise. Invite your children to help you set the schedule, as is appropriate. We tend to own those experiences in which we have a voice.
- **Pray *before* the prayer time.** A good friend suggests praying through the day for a successful family prayer time. When you consider the good fruit from even a seemingly average prayer time, it's well worth the investment of some prayer prep!
- **Communicate one on one.** Recently our teenaged daughter "rebelled" against family prayer. I got angry and asserted my "parental rights." After a tense evening and a restless night, I decided to listen instead of talk. I discovered my daughter had suffered from a headache due to lack of sleep, hence when it was time to pray she just didn't want to. We readjusted and the air cleared.

- **Something is better than nothing.** Some nights you may not get everyone to join in the family prayer. It's OK. Pray anyway. Sometimes your prayer time will be shortened. Pray anyway. Sometimes you won't feel particularly connected to God. Pray anyway. "When it's hardest to pray you must pray the hardest!"
- **Check your attitude.** One night at a Chinese restaurant my fortune cookie stated: *"No one is so wrong as he who thinks he is always right!"* I had gotten the wrong cookie–NOT! ☺ How is it that I can so easily move from a loving servant to a not-so-benevolent dictator?
- **Give the kids a chance.** My dad was devout, but rather opinionated! One year for Christmas I gave him a poster of a mobster surrounded by his hit men. The poster read: *"When I want your opinion, I'll give it to you!"* Enough said!
- **Rise and rise again, until lambs become lions.** Don't give up; even if you fall back for a while. Seek counsel if necessary, and try again.
- **Ask others to pray for you!** So important! As G. K. Chesterton said, "We are travelers together in a tiny lifeboat on a raging sea, and we owe one another a terrible loyalty." Get others to watch your back, spiritually speaking.
- **Surrender even this to God.** Saint Paul commands us, "In *all* circumstances give thanks, for this is the will of God for you in Christ Jesus" (1 Thessalonians 5:18).
- **Have a priest bless your home.** Perhaps there are spirits trying to harass you that somehow have become attached to your home, and need to be evicted! In Jesus' name, reclaim your home!

A FINAL WORD

The day was ending, a day like none other. So many people had tried to get near the Teacher that they were trampling one another underfoot. Power had gone out of Him, healing the blind, the lame, the mute. Devils had fled, screaming, from their victims. Pharisees and townspeople alike had challenged the Master, and now everyone had gone home.

Jesus looked at His disciples with compassion and love. "Do not fear, my little flock," He said with a gentle smile. "Your Father is pleased to give you the Kingdom. Seek His presence first, and everything else will be added unto you. Sell what you have and give to the poor, and provide for yourselves money bags that do not wear out, a treasure in heaven where neither thief nor moth can reach nor destroy. For where your treasure is, there will your hearts be."

Imagine that Jesus is standing before you now, smiling that same gentle smile. Your days are busy. He understands. Plans often go awry. He understands. Family members fight with each other; feelings get hurt. He understands. He walks over to you, places His hand on your shoulder, and says, "Do not fear, my child. Your Father knows that family life can be difficult. He has chosen you and each member of your family out of everyone ever created to belong to one another. Seek Him in prayer together. It is His good pleasure to give you eternal life, a life you can begin to share now, and will enjoy forever together in heaven. For where your family is, there will you find your heart."